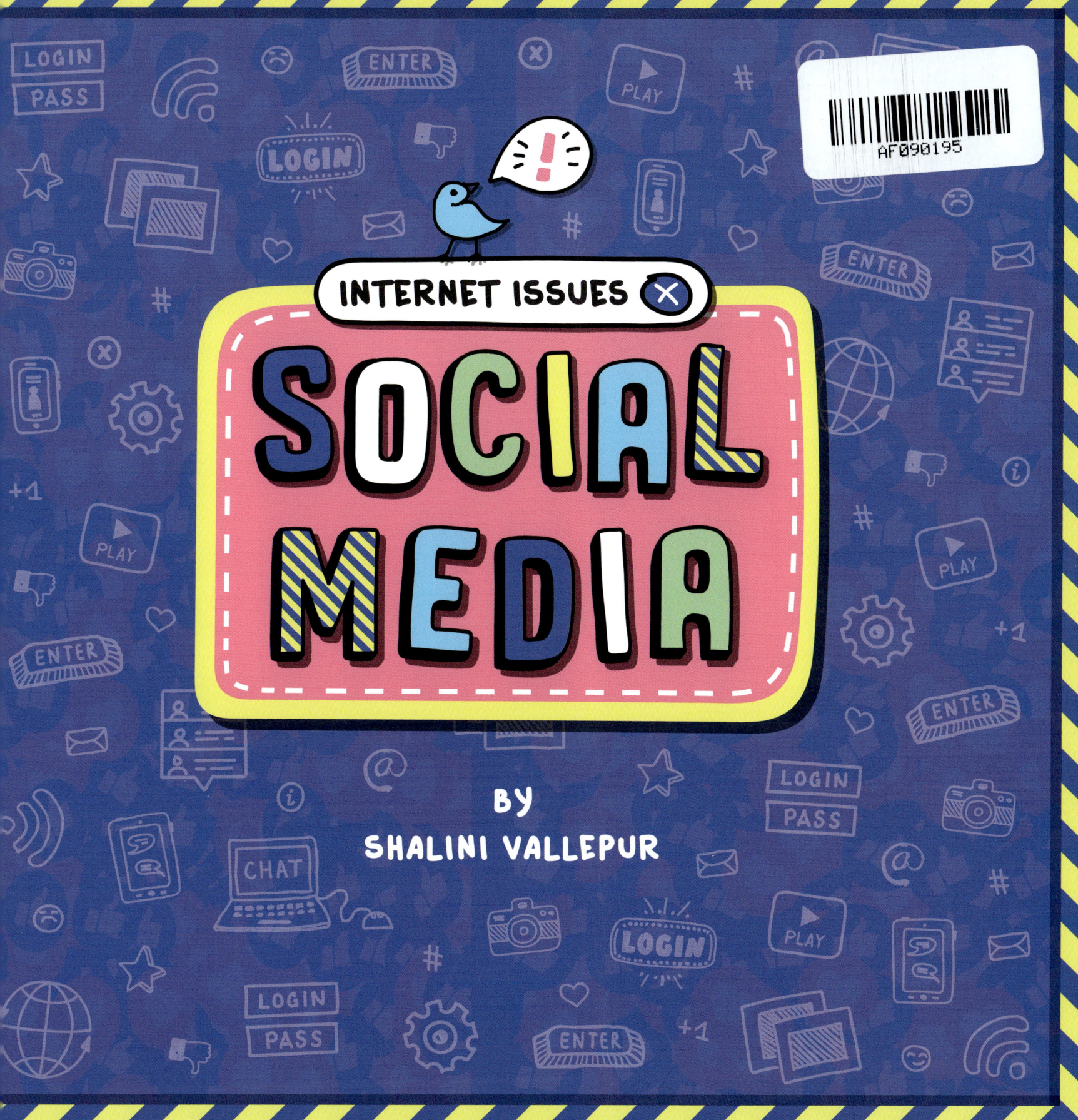

©2022
BookLife Publishing Ltd.
King's Lynn, Norfolk
PE30 4LS, UK

All rights reserved.
Printed in Poland.

A catalogue record for this book is available from the British Library.

ISBN: 978-1-80155-584-5

Written by:
Shalini Vallepur

Edited by:
John Wood

Designed by:
Danielle Rippengill

All facts, statistics, web addresses and URLs in this book were verified as valid and accurate at time of writing. No responsibility for any changes to external websites or references can be accepted by either the author or publisher

IMAGE CREDITS

All images are courtesy of Shutterstock.com, unless otherwise specified. With thanks to Getty Images, Thinkstock Photo and iStockphoto. Front Cover – Bloomicon, Alex Gontar, George Rudy, New Africa, Twin Design. Images used on every page – Bloomicon, Alex Gontar. 2 – Prostock-studio. 4–5 – fizkes, i_am_zews, Prostock-studio. 6–7 – Andrey_Popov, fizkes, szefei. 8–9 – Ostanina Anna, Prostock-studio, Sam72, wavebreakmedia wavebreakmedia. 10–11 – 13_Phunkod, Rahul Ramachandram, Robert Kneschke. 12–13 – fizkes, imtmphoto, Studio Romantic. 14–15 – Rawpixel.com. 16–17 – fizkes, Milles Studio, Monkey Business Images, New Africa. 18–19 – AnnGaysorn, Nigmatulina Aleksandra, Yalcin Sona. 20–21 – Odua Images, TheVisualsYouNeed, chainarong06. 22–23 – 24Novembers, Tyler Olson.

CONTENTS

PAGE 4	The Internet
PAGE 6	What Is Social Media?
PAGE 8	Different Devices
PAGE 10	Staying Safe
PAGE 12	Watching Videos
PAGE 14	Personal Information
PAGE 16	Photos and Friends
PAGE 18	Instant Messaging
PAGE 20	Cyberbullying
PAGE 22	Being Careful on Social Media
PAGE 24	Glossary and Index

WORDS THAT LOOK LIKE <u>this</u> CAN BE FOUND IN THE GLOSSARY ON PAGE 24.

THE INTERNET

Have you ever been on the internet? The internet links together computers, smartphones and tablets from all over the world. It lets computers connect with each other and share things.

People all over the world use the internet every day. The internet can be used for work, to learn, to play and to talk to other people.

OUR LIVES WOULD BE VERY DIFFERENT WITHOUT THE INTERNET.

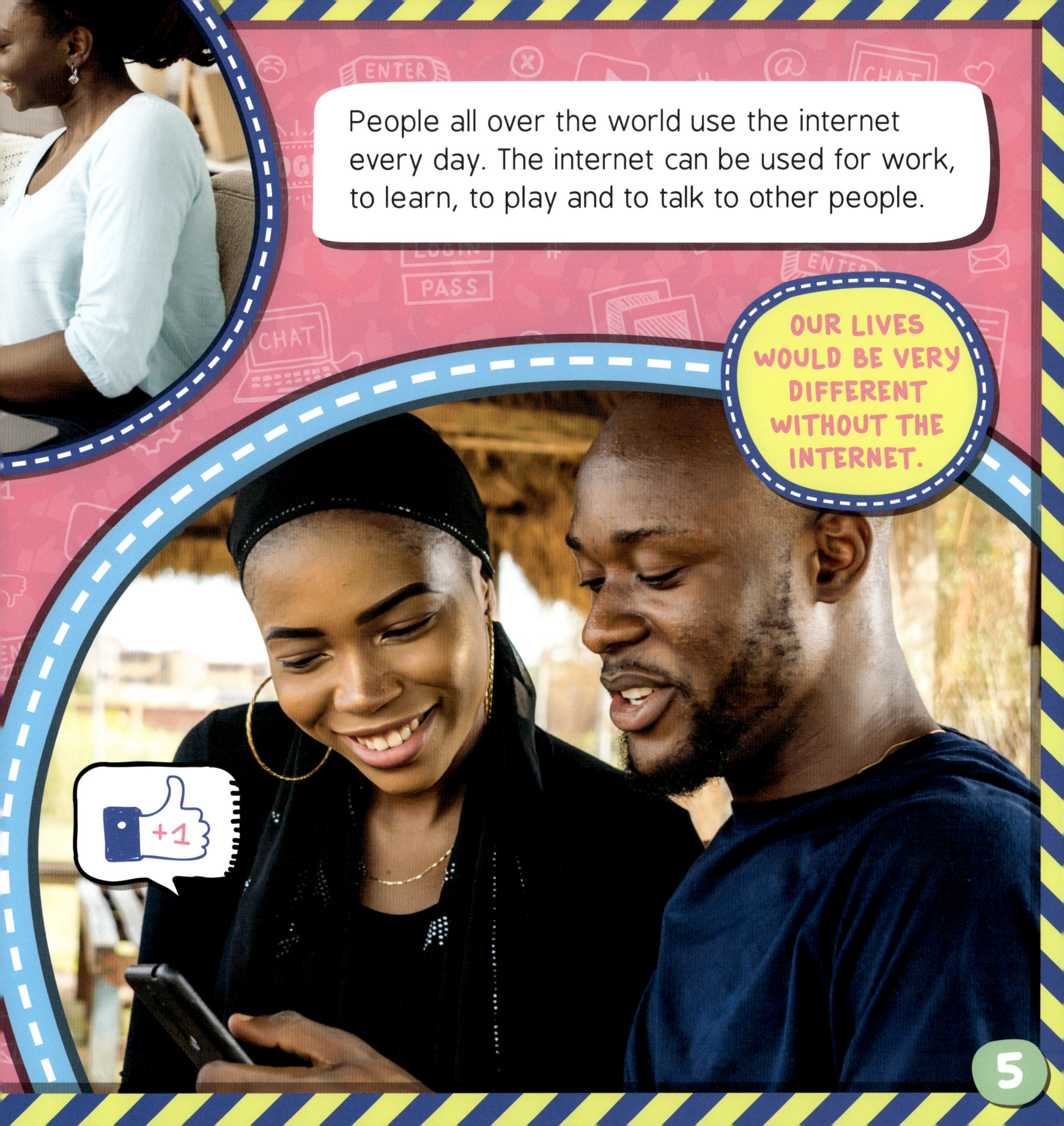

WHAT IS SOCIAL MEDIA?

When we talk about social media, we mean the **websites** and **apps** that let people talk and share things with each other. We often use social media to talk to people we trust and know in real life.

MOST SOCIAL MEDIA WEBSITES ARE MEANT FOR GROWN-UPS.

People can talk to their friends, share photos and watch videos on social media. While social media can be a lot of fun, it can also be dangerous. It's important to know how to stay safe.

Different DEVICES

Different **devices** can be used to go on the internet. Before going on the internet, it's important to check that your device's **security** settings are set up to protect you.

TABLET

SMARTPHONE

LAPTOP

ASK A GROWN-UP TO CHECK THE SECURITY SETTINGS ON ANY DEVICES THAT YOU USE.

IF YOU CLICK ON A POP-UP BY MISTAKE, JUST TELL A GROWN-UP!

Security settings can help stop harmful and dangerous things on the internet. Pop-ups can be harmful and they can appear on social media.

STAYING SAFE

Sometimes, people may pretend to be someone else on social media. To stay safe, it's important to only talk to people you know and trust.

ALWAYS ASK A GROWN-UP BEFORE YOU GO ON SOCIAL MEDIA.

When you go on social media or the internet, always make sure a grown-up is with you or nearby. You can also talk about being safe on social media with your teacher or other grown-ups.

Watching Videos

Some people share videos on social media. There are lots of fun videos to watch, such as TV shows, cartoons and music videos.

Some videos may show things that are meant for grown-ups. You might feel upset or unsafe if you see these kinds of videos. Talk to a grown-up if you see something that upsets you.

TRY USING A SOCIAL MEDIA WEBSITE THAT IS MEANT FOR CHILDREN.

PERSONAL INFORMATION

To go on social media, you may have to make an **account**. An account needs personal information. Here are some things that are your personal information:

- WHERE YOU LIVE
- YOUR USERNAME
- PASSWORD
- YOUR REAL NAME
- HOW OLD YOU ARE

NEVER SHARE YOUR PERSONAL INFORMATION WITH PEOPLE YOU DON'T KNOW!

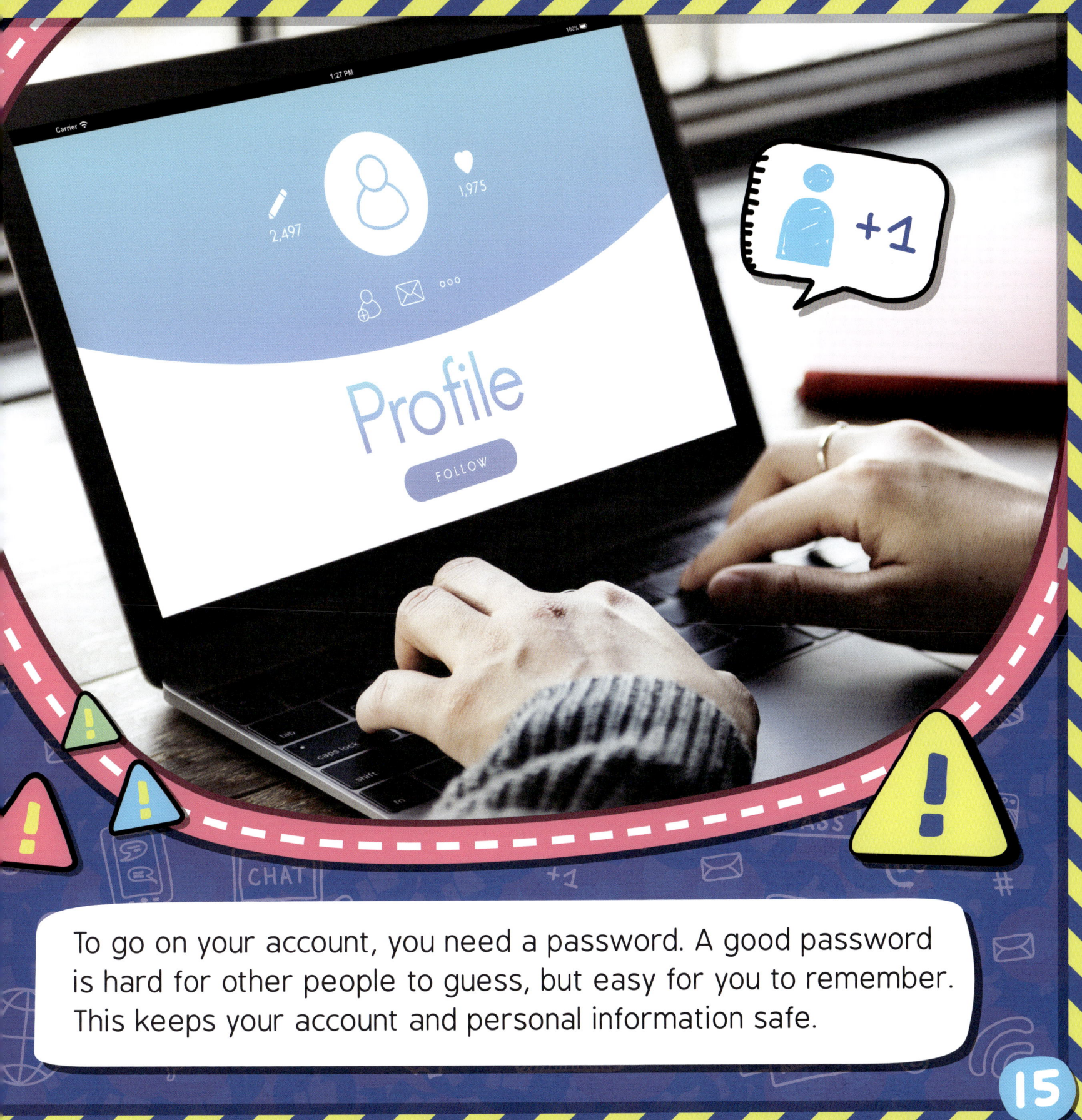

To go on your account, you need a password. A good password is hard for other people to guess, but easy for you to remember. This keeps your account and personal information safe.

PHOTOS AND FRIENDS

Adding friends on social media is fun! Sharing photos with friends is also a lot of fun, but when photos are posted onto social media, it can be hard to take them down.

CHECK WITH A GROWN-UP BEFORE YOU POST A PHOTO.

Even if you delete a photo, it may still be on the internet. Always be sure that you want to post something and never share mean or upsetting photos.

INSTANT MESSAGING

You can use many social media websites to send messages and call people you know. You can keep in touch with family and friends who live far away.

18

Be very careful about talking to somebody that you don't know in real life. Always check with a grown-up first.

DON'T SHARE YOUR PHONE NUMBER OR PERSONAL DETAILS WITH STRANGERS!

CYBERBULLYING

Talking to people on social media can be different to talking to them face-to-face. Cyberbullying is when bullying happens over the internet and it can be very upsetting.

CYBERBULLYING CAN HAPPEN TO ANYBODY.

DON'T SAY OR DO THINGS ON SOCIAL MEDIA THAT YOU WOULDN'T DO IN REAL LIFE.

Always be kind to other people on social media. If someone is unkind to you, or you see cyberbullying happening to someone else, tell a grown-up.

BEING CAREFUL ON SOCIAL MEDIA

Now you know all about social media! Let's go over how you can stay safe.

NEVER SHARE PERSONAL INFORMATION.

HAVE A GOOD PASSWORD THAT NOBODY CAN GUESS.

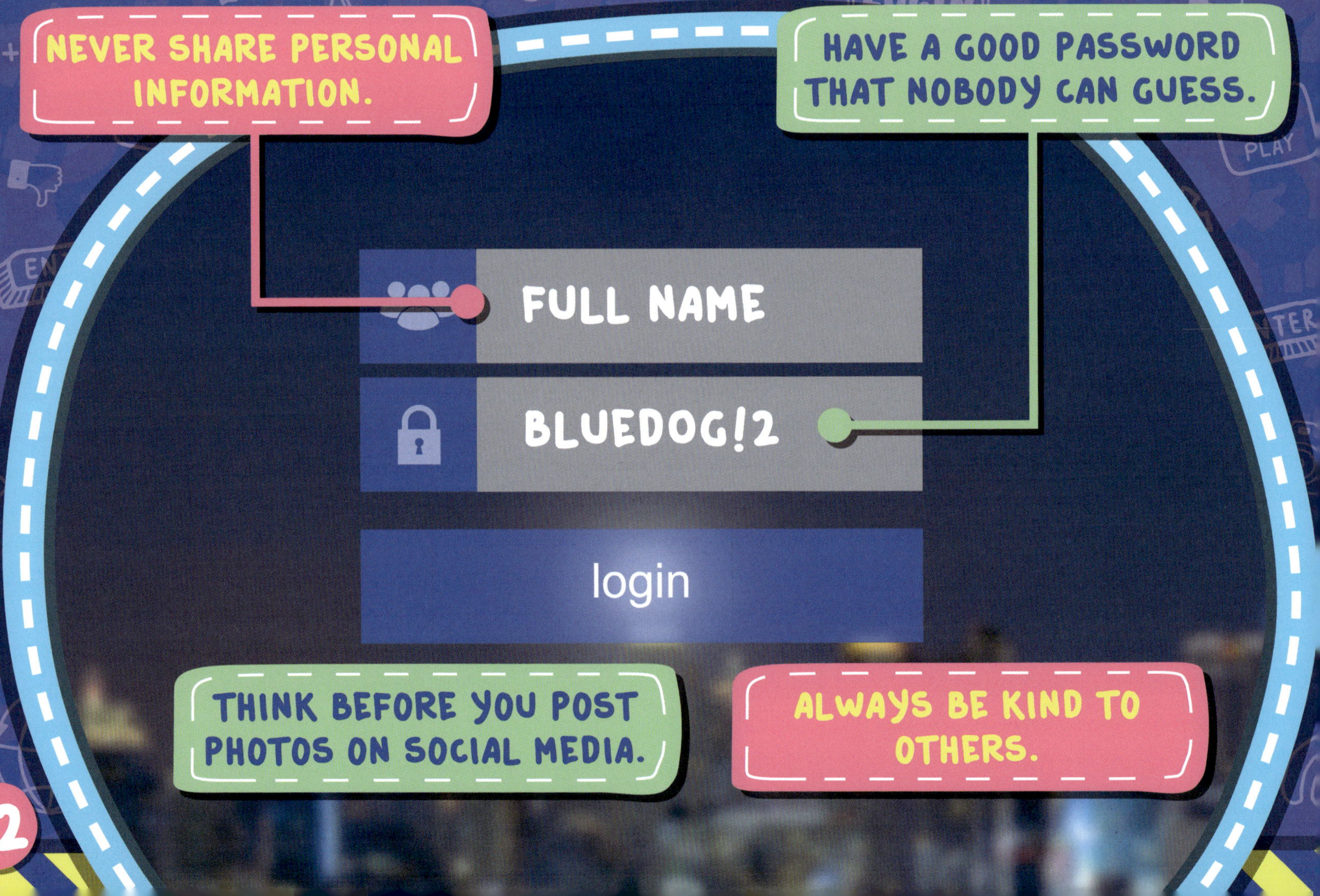

 FULL NAME

 BLUEDOG!2

login

THINK BEFORE YOU POST PHOTOS ON SOCIAL MEDIA.

ALWAYS BE KIND TO OTHERS.

GLOSSARY

ACCOUNT	part of a website or game that stores information about you that is used to get onto some parts of the internet
APPS	programs that work on mobile devices such as smartphones or tablets
DEVICES	electronic machines that are made for a particular purpose, such as smartphones, tablets, games consoles and computers
SECURITY	being protected or safe from harm
WEBSITES	parts of the internet that contain digital pages that are all linked together; they may contain a home page and other pages

INDEX

APPS 61
MESSAGES 18
PASSWORDS 14–15, 22
PERSONAL INFORMATION 14–15, 19, 22
PHOTOS 7, 16–17, 22
SECURITY 8–9
VIDEOS 7, 12–13